The Sleep of Reason

Morri Creech

WAYWISER

First published in 2013 by

THE WAYWISER PRESS

Bench House, 82 London Road, Chipping Norton, Oxon OX7 5FN, UK
P.O. Box 6205, Baltimore, MD 21206, USA
http://waywiser-press.com

Editor-in-Chief
Philip Hoy

Senior American Editor
Joseph Harrison

Associate Editors
Eric McHenry Clive Watkins Greg Williamson

ISBN 978-1-904130-53-6

Printed and bound by
T.J. International Ltd., Padstow, Cornwall, PL28 8RW

for Sarah

Acknowledgements

The following poems are dedicated to the following individuals: "Aubade" to Carol Wood; "Near Damascus" to Kevin Meaux; "Night Fire" to Hattie Creech; "Lullaby: under the Sun" to Miriam Creech; "The Trouble" to Steven Brown; "Song and Complaint" to Joseph Harrison; "The Perils of Art" to Michael Shewmaker; "Goldfinch", "The Choice," and "Depth of Field" to Sarah Creech; "Countryman of Bones" to Michael Livingston; "Heirloom: Nazi S. S. Cigarette Lighter" to D. W. Caison.

Thanks to the editors of the following magazines for publishing some of the poems included here: *32 Poems:* "The Choice"; *Columbia:* "Heirloom: Nazi S. S. Cigarette Lighter," "The Stone Well at Mt. Pisgah Church"; *First Things:* "Birch Trees in Sunlight," "Goldfinch," "Little Testament"; *Indiana Review:* "Apples of Recollection"; *Mead:* "Cold Pastoral"; *Measure:* "Night Fire," "By Noon Most Cunningly"; *New Criterion:* "Landfill," "Letter from the Coast," "The Trouble"; *Pembroke Magazine:* "Lullaby: under the Sun," "The Perils of Art"; *Sewanee Review:* "Banking Hours," "Depth of Field," "The Dream of Reason"; *Sewanee Theological Review:* "Late Reading"; *Southern Review:* "Song and Complaint"; *Southwest Review:* "Age of Wonders"; *Yale Review:* "Elegy for a Small Town Psychic."

"Depth of Field" was reprinted on *Poetry Daily* (online); "Depth of Field" and "Elegy for a Small Town Psychic" were reprinted in *Boomtown!* "Banking Hours" and "The Trouble" were reprinted in *The Swallow Anthology of New American Poets.*

"Night Blooming Cereus" was originally published in *Paper Cathedrals* (Kent UP 2001).

This book was written with the financial support of the National Endowment of the Arts, the North Carolina Arts Council, and Queens University of Charlotte; my sincere thanks to the individuals at those institutions who made that support possible, especially

Acknowledgements

Michael Kobre, Emily Seelbinder, and Lynn Morton. And my deepest gratitude to Kevin Meaux, Joseph Harrison, Susan Ludvigson, John Wood, Carol Wood, Dafydd Wood, Michael Shewmaker, William Trowbridge, Steven Brown, and Sarah Creech for their valuable attention and suggestions.

Contents

El sueño de la razón produce monstruos.

– Goya

The wild winds weep,
*   And the night is a-cold;*
Come hither, Sleep,
*   And my griefs infold:*
But lo! the morning peeps
*   Over the eastern steeps,*
And the rustling birds of dawn
The earth do scorn.

– William Blake

The Trouble

It seems these days you've had enough of order.
For months you harried the blackbirds from the yard
with a pellet gun, clatter of pie tins, an absurd
straw-stuffed overcoat, and gave no quarter,

chucking lit fireworks, once, to chase them off
the laundry poles and apple trees. And now?
The pump gun leans against the table saw
in your garage, the clean shirts billow and luff

in mild suburban peace, although the change
has quite unsettled you. It's true the lawn
looks clear, the trees untroubled. But at dawn
sometimes you hear the creaking of a hinge,

a swing set or a screen door, and you wake
thinking they might be there. Of course, they're not.
They loiter at the margins of your thought
like a dream you had once but can't seem to shake,

and now you wake so often that each time
wind sifts the limbs or flaps the empty sleeves
you want to tear them down, scatter the leaves
you spent all season raking into prim

heaps near the road, then stand out in the cold
beneath clouds of a slowly changing weather
and watch the pale sky darken to a feather,
until the meaning wings down and takes hold.

The Dream of Reason

For several minutes the whole drunken room
whirls in my half sleep, and a daze of motes
flares in spindrift galaxies, staggers and floats
like Descartes' dream, before the *ergo sum*
of consciousness calms the mind's delirium,
taking note of the room's coordinates–
floor and four walls where light accumulates;
the shade of blinds a slight wind moves at random.

What to make of this lingering trick of sense?
Descartes got up and, shaken from his ease
by a dance of sparks, a stranger, and a verse,
constructed from his thought firm evidence.

And me?
          Dust spins its bedlam universe
in my mind for days.
                         I'm tired of certainties.

Age of Wonders

January, 2011

Nel mezzo del cammin di nostra vita
– Dante

Old decade done, the morning throws off its shawl
of frost and the hedges drip with thaw water.
Like some postmodern Narcissus I stare at the pool
in my bathroom sink and pat my cheeks with lather
to scrape the aging face brisk, smooth, and pale;
beyond my window the persistent bother
of horns and engines – as early commuters rush
toward the shrines of commerce – drowns out Hardy's thrush

with the hope of goods and fortunes. Past forty now,
I lace my shoes and hit the Nordic track,
munch spoonfuls of bran and diced fruit, watch the Dow
streak past a flat screen rich with bric-a-brac
and sleek, tanned prophets who proclaim the Tao
of global markets, who's in, who's out, who's back
from jail, rehab, or chemo, while the snows
recede on Everest and the deficit grows.

What good is my pessimism? The soul completes
its journey in the dark and out of sight
or sulks the days in its tent of sinew, greets
the last hour happier than the first; but night
finds poor body cold on the chartered streets –
no point refusing him some warmth and light.
In T-shirt and shorts I sniff the heated air;
my Reeboks shuffle down a winding stair.

Still, something in me bristles. Is it age
merely, a dunderheaded sense the past
was better somehow – that glimmering mirage
glimpsed from a rearview mirror as the mist
ahead parts to reveal the yawning ledge
where the road should be, all distance closing fast?
Is it like that grumble before the gray
dandruff of history smothered out Pompeii?

Behind the bleach white sepulchers and smiles,
the lifted tits, twelve second abs, celebs
and pop stars tricked out in outlandish styles,
it flashes like a model's picket ribs
showing beneath her nightie where the aisles
crowd toward the check out and the bounty ebbs:
the sublime is out of joint, the ship has wrecked,
huge mounds of kitsch bury the intellect.

Not that one has much time to notice it,
fixed in some grimace of acceleration
(texting, say, on a highway late at night)
or savoring the popular elation
of Living in the Now – while skill and wit
go the old way of income, jobs, vacation,
savings accounts or the environment;
and nobody thinks to wonder where they went.

The shower steams up while the kettle shrieks.
When did the promise sour? I think of all
that didn't happen: the poems, books, and bucks,
freedom from the tyranny of dull
offices, projects, and bosses, and whole weeks
in cerebrotonic thought of the Ideal.
The present's proof (as has been said already)
that the future isn't what it used to be.

Mid-journey, though one of history's darlings still,
I pour my tea dregs down the drain and tie
the silk around my neck, mustering the will
to head for work. Trawling the squares of sky
trapped in my window frame, inevitable
for all their seeming randomness clouds go by
like traffic, brushed and freaked with pewter flaws,
obeying – as all things do – time's hidden laws.

By Noon Most Cunningly

All morning long I turned the morning over
in my head, the way a carpenter might think
about his notion of a perfect table.

The night's remains lay heaped beyond the sill.
I stood at the bay window in a bathrobe
drinking my coffee, looking out at the dark.

Then something penciled the lines and cut away
a few shapes from the formlessness. The spathes
of lilies, a lake, four birch trunks, a slate gray cloud.

The light meanwhile began to carve the shagged
bark of the birches – an elegant peeling scrollwork –
and carve the lilies' throats, the slender branches,

and then some fine tool smoothed the stars and moon
to an even blue and lathed the wrinkled lake
so the cloud and trees, joined, lay motionless there.

And that was the finished work: four straight birches
stilled on the water, lavish in their fixity
by the lilies, hefting a level slab of cloud.

The moment is well past now. It's nearing noon.
Anyone who cares to look can see the trunks
mottled with mold, the white caps, the restless sky.

Of course, I have that instance still in mind.
But the blades and lathes keep turning. Hour by hour
falls like sawdust swept from the maker's hands.

Landfill

Out here it's the same as ever – the rising piles,
the lined pits layered deep as Troy, and ditches
channeling drainage from the spent riches
that seem to stretch down the dirt road for miles:
flotsam of boxes, soup bones, scrap, the springs
coiling from sunk-in mattresses where dew
and rain have rosetted the stitching with mildew.
Inland seagulls hector with their wings
a strew of rinds and punctured bags. Beyond
the reeking mounds, bulldozers smooth the soil
over the sodden diapers and glittering foil
so that, as though some conjurer waved his wand
above a flat expanse of dust, you see
a little island looming at the edge
of vision: hairline of seedling grass, a ridge
with here and there a haggard maple tree,
the burlapped roots buried in beds of peat.
That place where Yeats thought all the ladders start?
At the heaps, a man steers a wobbly shopping cart
and throws in a pair of wing-tipped shoes, a sheet
of Visqueen, and what might be a megaphone
or tarnished trumpet – hard to tell. What brings
us back here? An ascetic's disdain for things,
or a hedonist's wish to claim them for his own?
A making-room-for-what-comes-next, the chair
in fashion from Ikea or Pier One
replacing the BarcaLounger, till we're done
with furniture and the house is sold, swept bare?
Meanwhile, on middle ground, we'll park the truck
to dump the armoire or the Frigidaire,
then stoop to appraise the treasure lying there
 – a necklace, broken-clasped yet bright as luck;
a fine-grained cherry table, its legs uneven –
though most leave with nothing. Kingdom of
the junked ham radio and gutted stove,

the whole place shimmers with flies, a feculent heaven
of stuff that's survived its use and, in some cases,
its users. Someone wore those wing-tipped shoes,
dozed on that mattress, read the *Daily News*
bundled and stacked there; surely there were faces
that stared from these empty frames. And if the past
outstrips the present, accumulating year
after year in bags and boxes, it ends up here,
the life that matters becoming the things that last.

Heirloom: Nazi S. S. Cigarette Lighter

Not quite a gift. Still, I have this from you:
stainless steel chased with runes and emblems, blue

flame stammering above twin etched letters. Each time
flint sparks a whiff of petrol, I think of numb

hands, neat and German, cupping its heat near
snow-cold Bastogne. In its bare light the year

is 1944. I watch you draw
a bead on the man's face suddenly aglow

from the startled cherry of his cigarette.
And then the flash when your two gazes meet

as, across the synapse of memory, I hear
its loud report in those stories from the war

you told drunk, thumbing the flint wheel. What does it mean
to handle dead men's fire that still burns clean

in the dark tonight? A spark. Then I see it all –
my face in the window, shadow on the wall.

Near Damascus

Old Saint Paul pulled the thorn from his side
& made theology of it.
God uttered a sound, & he rose from the ground
to that blind kingdom few men would covet.

Dream of the Pearl

One morning as he walked near the ocean a crowd gathered around him. "Tell us about the kingdom," they said. He picked up a shell from the beach and held it in his hand. Then he turned to them and said, "The kingdom is like a man who bought his neighbor's field after he found a pearl buried in it. For a long time the man sat looking at the pearl, admiring its luster and symmetry. But soon he grew afraid thinking others would come and want it for themselves so he buried it in the ground and built his house above it and hired guards to watch the house while he slept. Every night he dreamt the pearl was staring at him, but when he woke he couldn't recall what it looked like exactly. One morning the man hired musicians to sing songs about the pearl because he wanted to remember what he had dreamt. The first musician sang that the pearl was like the cold moon which shone down on everybody and governed the tides. The second sang that it was like a coin reflecting sunlight, which a man could hold inside his open palm. The third sang that it was a white excrescence formed around a sand grain trapped in an oyster shell. But the rest of them complained that it was useless to describe the pearl since they had never seen it, and soon they began to sing about other things. And the man grew restless because he wasn't sure what the pearl resembled. Now the musicians also knew about the pearl, and he drove them away from his door fearing they too would covet it. He bought up all of the fields surrounding his property so he could keep track of everyone who came near, and he hired more guards to patrol the perimeter of the house, and he locked the doors to keep even his servants out. And he stayed up pacing alone and staring out of his window at the stars burning in the heights and glaring up from the puddles in his field, and at the moon worn thin as a sliver in its blank socket. He never slept again."

Letter from the Coast

A brackish foam recalls
those summers here, a slur of mica specks
and glimmerings the sea drags back,
spume tossed up like a froth of pearl. Wet rocks
and a wharf's pilings lather in the slack
tide, where a few gulls brawl.

Beyond the pier, you stretched
full-length on a beach towel, propped on elbows, thumbing
a novel or a magazine.
It's summer still. Waist deep, the ocean's numbing
at first, and sun-blind as it's always been,
the sand dunes etched

and scalloped by crosswinds
that wrinkle the sea's reflection. Cloud, birds, sun
warp and skew in a funhouse mirror
of tilting water; and the years have done
much the same trick – or else the past seems clearer,
as if perspective bends

the present out of shape,
poor copy of the mind's pure paradigm.
For instance, who remembers the Hyatt
shading the sea oats down shore, or that slime
on the beached keels? *Let me find a little quiet,*
you said, and the seascape

has done just the opposite,
by God – more bathers, plunderers of shells
and shark's teeth, couples linking hands;
more noisy kids with kites, buckets, and shovels.
Still, the sea doesn't change much. Here are the sands
where you used to sit

watching the tide retreat –
or, anyway, they look the same. And all
the lovely houses built on sand
echo those summers, too, identical,
receding into the distance, inching inland,
as the waves repeat, repeat.

Aubade

At daybreak light falls
through a thin gap in the curtains
like meaning drawn tight on a shivering thread.

It sews to my screen the amber
husk of a damselfly
then spindles down as an axle around which turn
loose planets and a thousand burning
filaments of dust.

Beyond the scrim a world ravels to pure dream –
chaos of bare branches, havoc of red
birds preening themselves like theories in a tree
in Berkeley's forest.

What dreams me – hair uncombed, unshaved and slippered,
sweeping my hand through harp strings of light
to sound some dumb
gimcrack music of the spheres?

The light is altering now. When I pull the cord
sun looms at the sill
where leaves spin their intricate equations
and a red bird knows my shadow.

It cocks its head at me, then flares
like a shuttle of fire from the hedge to the honey locust
between my dazed reflection and the day.

Song and Complaint

Thou wast not born for death, immortal Bird!
– John Keats, "Ode to a Nightingale"

I

Beat it, bird. We've heard enough about
     the charms of elsewhere. While you poured forth your soul
like a poet hidden in the light of thought,
     blithe spirit, we grew tired of the whole
immortal business; each of us has drunk
     from the cup of sorrows and of boredom, too.
          So I've wandered out here onto the front lawn
               half-dressed, picked up a chunk
of gravel, and I'm aiming it at you.
     A nice tune, but we'd rather you were gone.

II

Most mornings here I take the trash outside
        and haul it to the curb. I know you're there –
a twitch in the mock orange, not to be denied,
        persistent as a dream or a nightmare.
And, once, I carried the bag out the back door
        surrounded by a crush of flies, and heard
                a fluttering. I looked up but couldn't see
                the sky. Next thing, a snore.
My own. I'd dreamt the trash, the flies, the bird.
        It felt like the wing of madness over me.

III

I remember how in childhood I dreamed of
    the nothing brimming in that gulf of shade
beyond the lights. A mockingbird or dove
    at evening shook a dogwood branch and made
some kind of sound, and then I knew for sure
    matter didn't end there in the dark.
        The world went on. I didn't have to guess
        whether the noon flowers were
somewhere. But you – thrush, nightingale, or lark? –
    bring back that first desire for emptiness.

IV

You're tempting, bird. We'd all like to believe
    in a vast perfection – to imagine France
without the guillotine, or Adam and Eve
    beneath the boughs without their underpants;
to sleep at four a.m. without the noise
    of car alarms or breaking glass. One time
        I heard your voice and caught the scent of clover
        on the night air, and the joys
of oblivion brushed my cheek. It was sublime.
    Then a slammed door woke me like a hangover.

V

Procne or Philomela? I forget.
    I read the story in eleventh grade.
Even in high school, though, they rarely let
    kids in on things like that – the rapist's blade,
the severed tongue and tapestry. We want
    the song without the bloodshed. Now you've come
        full-throated, cheerful, with your small wings furled,
            whistling as if to taunt
my ignorance. But I'd prefer you dumb.
    The world you sing about is not the world.

VI

It's possible to say you don't exist.
    I've never seen you. Are you a conclusion
dressed down in plain clothes by a theorist,
    like anti-quarks, the Trinity, or cold fusion?
Who knows. Your singing's comforted a few.
      Bonhoeffer in his cell. Kings, clowns, and Ruth.
        Mostly, though, it seems you're like the gap
        a child's tongue wiggles through
for days and days after he's lost a tooth,
    or the midnight drip of water from the tap.

VII

Like a flute's trill in the distances of air
    heard at a crucifixion, a plane crash,
or some terrible *Exeunt, chased by a bear,*
    your anthem grates. Time and the music clash.
You sang at Gettysburg and Waterloo.
    You sang while Caesars held Rome by the ears
        and the pick burrowed into Trotsky's skull.
        Through plagues you sang and flew,
trials, inquisitions, a whole age of tears.
    Our history now seems oddly musical.

VIII

I've thrown my rock, bird. And, now that you're gone,
    I'd like to go inside and get some sleep.
It's been a long night, after all. Soon dawn
        will wade through shadows on the yard and steep
the trees in sunlight, and the window blinds
    will slant the bedclothes and my dreaming face.
        Who'll grieve your music in some fit of rhyme
        or keep you in our minds
now that it's so damned quiet? Maybe I'll pace
    and listen awhile. As long as I have time.

Lullaby: Under the Sun

My daughter, sprawled out on her blanket,
turns over once, then dozes off.
She knows that there is time enough.
Above, the sun bobs like a trinket
  through a vagrant scrim of cloud
  that softens noon to a green shade.

Tempting, to sentimentalize
a day like this, a child this small –
no humming gnats or sparrow's fall,
no thunderhead crowding the skies
  to mar the general accord;
  while God looks on, profoundly bored.

Elsewhere, of course, it's business
as usual: the sweet and sour
of passion, preemptive acts of power,
some Passchendaele or Austerlitz
  that has or hasn't happened yet
  and history will soon forget.

I've read too many books. I've seen
towers toppled, regimes dragged down;
seen heads of state raised to renown
while war planes strafed the TV screen.
  The crooks who caused the market crash
  resign with pocketfuls of cash.

And yet the *carpe diem* theme
is old as either love or war.
It will all go on as it has before –
an idiot's tale, a play or dream.
  My daughter sleeps. Made on such stuff
  the lovely world seems true enough.

Elegy for a Small Town Psychic

Weekdays you rummaged through the universe
    spinning around inside your crystal ball
for Lotto numbers, the checkout girl's lost purse,
    some plumber's vagrant niece who wouldn't call.
    Alas, the turban and the sequined shawl
are all packed up now with your uncashed checks,
sandalwood incense, candles, tarot decks.

The past is where we left it – swept away
    under some cosmic couch or coffee table
where, fuzzed with lint, it will most likely stay.
    Who will reclaim for us, Clairvoyant Mabel,
    those trivial hours, and polish them to fable –
the New Year's kiss, the wealthy man's dropped glove
we might have turned to money or to love?

And the future? Time grinds forward on its track,
    keeping to schedule though you've stepped off board.
Great sage of horoscope and zodiac,
    nine hundred number, palm, and credit card
    – prophet the constellations once adored –
who will conduct us now on our destined way?
The tight-lipped stars have nothing left to say.

The Choice

What chose us? Just as well to ask what chose
the chinaberry and wild olive and close-
cropped weeds in the friend's yard where we met
or the noise and traffic of whatever street
had brought us there. Wind made the pattern of
the yellow sundress you were wearing move
a little, in a larceny that took
possession of the light and made me look.

You spoke. Or else I did. The past is fiction.
But I can say whatever dereliction
of purpose conjured us together here
in these changing roles that suit us every year
we choose it as our own again tonight
beneath the lucid tyranny of starlight.

Birch Trees in Sunlight

Though the clear morning stood
        composed – cloud, dew, and leaf,

the whole shimmering wood –
        now it all seems past belief.

We know what happened. How
        a man came with his camera

to take these stills of bough
        and branch. The old chimera

of harder days had gone
        underground. But what brought

him here was not the dawn
        light, the tall trunks caught

in chiaroscuro, or
        twigs dense as tangled thread.

He'd seen these woods before.
        Now past and present wed

the way, in textbooks, bone
        at one turn of the page

will suddenly have grown
        nerve, muscle, and cartilage,

those intricate details
        obscuring what was there.

How to weigh these in the scales
        – moss, lichen, the pure air –

with what we've already seen:
                the fluttering rags, those drawn-

faced children beneath the lean
                birches that earlier dawn?

Just so, the story ends
                laved clean in August sun.

And still the mind contends
                with what can't be undone:

thick, sun-shot canopies
                billowing overhead

and, under the Polish trees,
                those faces of the dead –

how beauty and brute fact
                here buckle, overlaid

in snapshots, each exact,
                in brilliance and in shade.

Restoration

Who greets your mirrored gaze?
It seems the Janus face
of time this once has turned
from the past and future's haze
to stare straight at itself.
The letters that you burned,
restored now, take their place
again on the high shelf;

the boulders and the scree
have rolled back up the mountain,
restitched to the stone's side.
The old face that you see,
the young rake standing tongue-tied
in front of the Trevi Fountain
– both halves, before and after –
meet for now in laughter.

Look, here you are in steerage
staring out at the sea
from a fogged, oval window –
thirteen maybe. And there
you are in your last marriage.
Now you're throwing a key
down a well. Now you remember
someone you don't yet know.

There's a lighthouse. Dawn. The sound
of change jingling in a pocket.
Black hair, a rumpled dress.
Your father – or is that you? –
with his arms wrapped around
a woman in a locket.
There's a book, a game of chess,
a panther at the zoo.

It's only they who stand
here listening to you – amazed
as you recount so clearly
what happened or what will –
it's they who seem erased.
Meanwhile it's late. It's early.
A boy grips the sill
but with a spotted hand.

And the days spin their thread.
For a while memory holds
the pins between her lips
and spreads out like a cloud
the whole cloth, smoothing the folds
to show the seamless years,
before her fingers slip
and then it disappears.

Late Reading

The question the lamp illuminates is whether
or not to ask the question. The young prince
pacing the battlements and the girl waist deep
in riverweed will soon enough become
the fool's skull pondered by a later age.
And if the blank white sockets make us wince?
There is, after all, still time to turn the page,
to have a cup of tea or get some sleep
or simply close the big book altogether –
each, in its way, an answer to the question;
though whether the reader falls for the deception
of a pearl dropped in a cup or savors some
nobler design – swords brandished in a rage –
the last act always sees its kingdom come.

The Stone Well at Mt. Pisgah Church

No draught from heaven here. The well, though, is
an open eye that peers at marsh hawks passing
over, the brown spider hard at her hieroglyphics
spanning the stones. It takes all in and gives
up nothing. I gaze down that cool funnel
where noon light contracts to a dazzled pupil.
Once, they dropped a man in, windlass rope
tight as a needle's eye around his throat.
He twitched a minute or so. Then grew still.
Now history here shrinks to a lidless socket
hoarding an image of the cloudy spire.
Serene in its reflection, it makes no comment
but holds me, too, in its regard, the bucket
a tongueless bell poised over the soundless dark.

The Perils of Art

I

Christ crucified, or Goya's madhouse, ox
trussed in a butcher's shop in browns and reds –
my niece would rather turn
the page to see the Virgin of the Rocks,
satyrs and nymphs, or one of Renoir's nudes.
She's nine. She won't learn

the rigors or the thrills of the sublime
for a while I guess; and ours is a quick tour
from Giotto to Magritte
on a rainy afternoon to pass the time.
She likes Rococo, smiling de La Tour,
the images of sweet

tamed nature. What she doesn't understand
 – and what I'm at a loss here to explain –
is why the painter's gaze
turns from the quaint, the picturesque, the grand
(fauns, landscapes, gods) to sacrifice and pain,
as if that urge betrays

a monstrous something in the artist's mind.
Maybe. And it may be years before she knows
what monster waits at the heart
of the labyrinth. Besides, to her the world looks kind.
Pop music. Girl-meets-boy. The rest is noise.
Nothing to do with art.

II

My friend, a professional photographer,
takes nature photos mostly: black-and-whites
of oak trees, resurrection fern, the dusk
sunlight hanging above the jasmined fences
and tangled gardens of Louisiana.
He makes a modest living. People want
assurances, which they can frame as truth.
So who else but he would understand
why, when his son was struck by a passing car
and sprawled beside the road – and as my friend
waited for the ambulance to arrive,
not knowing yet whether his son would live –
he ran back to the house, fetched his camera,
and took shot after brilliant shot of what
lay splayed there in the grass, as still as art.

III

What is it, the old need
to set things down, record
a hurt child in the weeds,
the Horatii's raised swords,

Christ lowered from the cross –
what draws the eye again
to violence and loss?
The boy is nearly ten.

My friend has never shown
him the photographs he took.
Sometimes when he's alone
he'll take them from his book,

glance once, then put them back.
They're beautiful, he tells
me, more than the gimcrack
pictures he frames and sells.

So what do I tell my niece –
that things conceived in terror
eclipse some works of peace?
that vision redeems the error?

Here she is, in these lines
with flashbulb and wounded child,
though the story isn't mine
and nothing's reconciled.

We look. More pages turn.
Medusa's lost her head,
Turner's ships still burn,
Marat slumps forward, dead ...

Paint brush or camera lens.
It's no easy trick, the art
of knowing where horror ends,
and where the beauty starts.

Goldfinch

Carel Fabritius. 1654, oil on panel, 35.2 cm. x 22.8 cm.

The bird is fiction though the paint is real –
the paint, that is, of the original.

This one's a copy pasted in a frame.
Each hour the gold light on his wall's the same.

He hangs between the cupboard and the fridge
where, day after day, it is his privilege

to see our windowed sunlight come and go,
eavesdrop on music from the stereo,

mark my ditherings or eye my bathrobed wife.
I think he'd trade his stillness for my life,

just as I often envy him his stasis.
O plump brown household god, what most amazes

is how, held in that perfect light from Delft,
chained to a narrow rail, perched on a shelf

in 1654, you look at us –
small finch that might have watched Fabritius

the year flame rendered him to ash. You stare
from a modest trompe l'oeil heaven we don't share.

Mute bird, they're finite, as you know, the days.
But sing to us. Sing of the light that stays.

Little Testament

Sure as that first command which strung the light
like thread onto a loom
to stitch the finished tapestry of sight,
he flips a switch and instantly the room
reweaves its intricacies
of warp and weft: chair canted against the wall,
nightstand strewn with coins and papers, shawl
draping one lamp whose shadow like a stain
has inched up to the brink
of his rucked sheets, over the herringbone grain
and knots of hardwood where he sees
the nicks and scuffs no brilliance can appall.

Soon he will shuffle down the hall
past photos of his elsewhere son and daughter
to lean over the face of the gray water
dappled with lather in the bathroom sink,
then round the narrow stairs
to where – tie brushing the granite countertop –
he will raise the bounty of his coffee cup
and break his crustless toast alone,
foreseeing the martyrdom of that day's affairs:
the dolorous road to work, the bills and rent.

But now, not risen yet, before the sun
unwinds its bolt of bullion
in his curtained room, and the accomplishment
of circuitry and wattage gets outshone
by simpler majesties – before
the music of the spheres (shrunk on an iPod
docked to his stereo)
tangles itself in the raucous, louder score
of trash truck sirens, horns and brakes galore,
and harrowed shouts below –
why shouldn't he pronounce the morning good,

this god of modest testaments and decrees,
of lesser verities
dutifully loved if dimly understood?

Night Blooming Cereus

Photograph, "King of the Night," by Cy DeCosse

What should we say of them, these lush, moon-scented
blossoms that memorialize the light?
Say they gather the night against themselves,
cast in bold relief on the bare-lit world.

Or else say they are nothing like those flowers
your mother picked among the tattered rows
each summer, roses and the flushed petals
of lilies sharing their brilliance with the sun's.

One version of the story is that God,
having forged the world, allowed no other gods
to share that newly made magnificence.

Say these, then, are the flowers made in His image,
kings of the night that, raging in the dark,
shall suffer no light fiercer than their own.

That Old Time Religion

And he said, "To what should I compare the kingdom? It is like several men who coveted a neighbor's possessions. They broke in one evening and stole everything he owned, setting fire to his house as they went away. Now when they returned to their own land they invested the man's possessions wisely so they were able to build lavish mansions, each of them, and live in peace. One night after many years had passed they were enjoying a dinner party in the finest mansion when suddenly a hush fell over them. Each time they sipped their highballs or stretched out on the plush chairs and couches they smelled smoke. Over the sumptuous dishes their eyes watered. The beef wellington tasted of ash. Even the caviar smacked of cinders and char. Finally a few of them decided to go outside, champagne flutes in hand, to see what was the matter. And they saw that fire had consumed everything between their own mansions and the neighbor's land, and now it was threatening the edges of their manicured lawns. One of the men, a respected religious leader, sickened by the smoke, grew indignant and denounced it as evil. Another, a senator, suggested they write legislation prohibiting anyone from setting fires. Yet another man, a builder, said they should construct a high wall between themselves and the fire so at least they wouldn't have to look at it. Some men proposed going indoors and stuffing the doorjambs with towels and lighting incense, while others in loud voices blamed the neighbor for building a house out of such flammable material. Perhaps, someone said, they should charge him for not stopping the fire from spreading. A few tossed champagne onto the fire and then fell to congratulating themselves. But at midnight, grown weary at last, they each went home to dream their private dreams. And the ashes came down and smothered them and they never woke."

Banking Hours

Time to get down to business. Time to settle
accounts and round the sums.
The sun's loose change lies scattered on the floor
and shade has inched between the pansies and the mums.
The piper's all played out, the whore's been diddled,
and the shops have closed their doors.

Time to square with the clock's big jaundiced eye
as it glares back at you;
with those two sweeping hands that meet like shears
when you wake up not sure yet if the dream was true.
Time to answer the phone and tell us why
your payments are in arrears.

Time to admit the check was never "in
the mail," that you were never
"between jobs currently," nor was your card
mischarged, stolen, lost. You've always been so clever.
You've always had a tendency to spend
more than you could afford.

How easily you fall for cheap distractions:
long nights, gossip and girls,
the highball tumbler sweating along its facets.
How easily, old swine, you fritter away your pearls
for one more chance to nose the world's confections,
squandering your assets

until, look, it's late; the leaves have gone the way
of dames and dollars now.
The spider's tallied up her last gauze beads
on the web strung between the porch and locust bough.
That wind sounds like the rake of a croupier
combing the yellow weeds.

So run the spreadsheets. Balance the register.
You knew, of course – didn't you? –
the bill would post, that notice for both prime
and principal: Records Show. Please Pay Amount Due.
It's time to make good with your creditor.
Soon ends will meet. It's time,

dear customer, it's time.

Countryman of Bones

Michael, what of this river where
the stars lie scattered here and there
like jacks tossed on linoleum
and left after a finished game,
wind wrinkling those waters stretched
from bank to bank that, finely etched
with the moon's faint strokes from overhead,
glimmer with all we might have said?

Some old Greek knew this place to be
all time needs of philosophy –
although, of course, he never stood
near this particular seaward road
watching his own reflection stay
while limbs and leaves hurried away
downstream to wash up God knows where.
And, truth be told, you didn't care

much for the jabbering in books,
preferring to jackknife from the rocks
and thrash around a little while
in the strong current. It's just as well.
Words fail anyway, grown hoarse
with worn-out feeling or – what's worse –
cloying with the confections of
sentiment. Well, you had enough.

Besides, what words or waters reach
across the blinding miles to fetch
you back now? Umpteen tons of sand
slipped through a narrowing glass to land
you on some road where a Humvee spins
wildly toward our public ends.
Nothing can negotiate
such distances. It's getting late.

Better to dwell on other things –
the moon-slicked river, osprey wings
rowing across the empty air
beyond the Baptist church's spire
where once a week for fifteen years
we both sang hymns and made our prayers
to God and those eternal laws
that are themselves effect and cause,

or the warped pier where, classes done,
we'd worship the oblivion
of whiskey, Zeppelin, pungent hash
bought two miles out beyond the marsh
but grown in some exotic place
whose desolation makes our peace,
then strip our shirts and disappear
in black depths to resurface here

where I look now. In a different year.
Things are much as they were before –
headlights solve the general dark,
kids still come here to neck and park
their cars, stoke fires in trashcans, grow
up as we once did years ago,
full of the same boredom and rage
that dead-end, or dull to middle age.

Too old for childish stuff, I'll drive
home bored and angry (still alive
that is) past banks, schools, hardware stores,
these houses that our foreign wars
keep safe, and, one of the elect,
lie down to sleep, my doors unlocked
while night – far from all harsh alarms –
takes the republic in its arms.

On Corporate Money as Political Speech

To those broken men who barter every good
not to be heard is to be understood.

Cold Pastoral

The nightingale to Keats

I

Much have I traveled. The gold sun sinks to dark
    behind the trees of Hampstead Heath where you
incline your head to listen for the lark
    or linnet, birds whose songs are mostly true.
Now – although nothing swims into your ken –
    you hear a distant singing that you think
        has sought you out. It happens that you're right.
        Sweet as a Lethean wine,
rich as the dram which one day soon you'll drink
    on a Roman road to toast the coming night.

II

Go on and write this down if you feel like it.
    It won't turn out the way you want it to.
For all you know, posterity will strike it
    from the page whose permanence is like the blue
revisions of the surf off Margate's coast.
    I am a figment of the song you scrawl
        on a stave of pain, an absence in the air
            you've fixed a name to – lost
somewhere between the true and beautiful,
    those poles more separate than sea and star.

III

Like "one that gathers Samphire dreadful trade"
    (another hand has helped write your letter)
you lean toward the emptiness where music's made
    to follow me. Who wouldn't shake the fetter
of imitation loose to find himself?
    Far down that ledge you're slowly climbing over
    I hover and hover, winging the abyss –
        it's a sheer drop from that shelf
of stone. Beyond my voice, these pines and clover,
    an inland sea keeps breaking. The waves hiss.

IV

And you wake to the next stage of the dream.
    You don't know where you are. Cheapside? Gravesend?
That room where limbs twitch in a pail, the scream
    of an injured man no surgery could mend
thundering like a pulse? You're far away,
    listening to a landscape you can't see
        because I'm singing it. The childhood stalls,
        Tom's foaming cough, the gray
London streets bloom as thicket, flower, and tree,
    on which I let these fictive feathers fall.

V

What voice is true enough? Aye, there's the rub.
    The words you use to conjure up a world
are like the scent of flowers to mask the grub
    you'll choke down on the long road. Wings unfurled,
I'm whistling on a bough of pure invention.
    Imagination's underside is death,
        a vast reality that's coming true
            in your speech's spoiled intention,
in every hope that won't outlast your breath
    whose sound not even poetry can renew.

VI

One fact is that the singer always dies –
    the effect of which you're naturally aware.
Or will be. But listen with a wild surmise
    to this one, too: all song is only air,
strokes on a page, an ink stain's coiling mischief
    the years dissolve and others quite forget.
        Once the branch is still, the sound is gone,
        the ink in the well dries stiff,
and the editor has withheld his final *stet*,
    who will be there to tell me where I've flown?

VII

Here. Rome. Your window. 1821.
　　Severn has wiped your brow and serves you tea.
Your whole life cramps into a room for one.
　　Still dreaming of some undiscovered country!
Just look how it unfolds inside your mind –
　　vibrant as violets and the eglantine
　　　　of Hampstead Heath, the Queen Moon, or the choirs
　　　　　　you gathered from the wind
stirring beneath my vans into one fine
　　note held between the shadows and the stars.

Dirge at Evening

Then silence dragged a gray wing over St. Helena Sound –
the only white noise ten gaunt black birds
scratching the graveled ground.

Apples of Recollection

Once, stumbling into the twilight kitchen, drowsy, leaning above
the ripe fruit on the countertop, hearing only a moth thump
against the fluorescent light and a slight breeze swell the curtains,
I had a vision. There was a long path down to the apple trees

my grandfather grafted when he was young. They shed their leaves
in the cold light. I walked there and found my father, twenty six,
bent on a ladder, hoisting a half-full bucket toward the boughs.
The sunlight fell in columns through the biggest branches.

I knew somehow that my mother had been gone five months,
and still he picked apples for the pies she would never make.
One fell groundward and rolled toward my feet. I was sure
that if I picked it up, if I lifted it to my mouth and took a bite,

I would remember nothing of what I saw. And for a time
there was nothing else, just that moment, a father busy at work
among the trees, plucking the swollen apples no one would eat,
and his child below him, holding the one piece of fruit

he was strictly forbidden, for memory's sake, to taste. All of this
might pass through the gates of ivory in an instant.
And then I woke. I stood there alone in the fluorescent light
of the present, in the kitchen, holding the unbitten apple in my palm.

Night Fire

I struck the match. My child watched dead leaves burn
and catch the crib of twigs, and watched me turn
the callow cinders with an alder stick
until, in time, bright specks whirled in the thick
overhead branches so you couldn't tell
which were the sparks and which the stars, and all
around us shadows intricately wrought
swayed fiercely against the absolute of night.

What's left this morning? Ashes and a round
of stones, two unsplit oak logs on the ground,
a child asleep, and all the mind remembers.

Yet there it is: her face in a daze of embers,
that weave of limbs against a farther sky,
the fire of language I still see them by.

Depth of Field

The web looks cluttered with particulars:
filaments rain-strung like an abacus;
some bits of grit; wings in mismatched pairs
around a desiccated carapace;
a bright leaf blown loose from the hawthorn hedge.
The spider tiptoes at one raveled edge.

Or else taps on its wires a shining morse
our sight translates until the world assembles
and, shaken, holds. The daylight's downward course,
reflected on each wet thread, hangs and trembles.
The scattered trees, those far hills, to the eye
seem gathered there and gleam like tesserae.

Both a frame and object, then, for our regard.
Through the shells of dead bees stippling that lens
you glimpse live bees carousing in the yard,
stumbling among the waxbells and impatiens.
You see the puzzled clarity of the web,
the round sun's spoked refraction and its ebb.

But let the observer go home, let him sleep,
dreaming of bee and web, leaf and sun
 – parts of that finished day the mind will keep,
spinning those several visions to the one –
while the spider, lost among the vanished trees,
looms its inscrutable geometries.

A Note About Morri Creech

Morri Creech was born in Moncks Corner, South Carolina, USA, in 1970 and was educated at Winthrop University and McNeese State University. He is the author of two previous collections of poetry, *Paper Cathedrals* (Kent State University Press, 2001) and *Field Knowledge* (Waywiser, 2006), which received the Anthony Hecht Poetry prize and was nominated for both the *Los Angeles Times* Book Award and the Poet's Prize. A recipient of NEA and Ruth Lilly Fellowships, as well as grants from the North Carolina and Louisana Arts councils, he is the Writer in Residence at Queens University of Charlotte, where he teaches courses in both the undergraduate creative writing program and in the low residency M.F.A. program. He lives in Charlotte, North Carolina with his wife and two children.

Other Books from Waywiser

Other Books from Waywiser